TRACK
is for me

TRACK
is for me

Lowell A. Dickmeyer

photographs by
Alan Oddie

 Lerner Publications Company   Minneapolis

The author wishes to thank the coaches and participants at the Newbury Park Athletic Association; Joyce Parkel, track coach at Oxnard College; and Ray Estrada and other personnel of the Oxnard Athletic Association.

LIBRARY OF CONGRESS CATALOGING IN PUBLICATION DATA

Dickmeyer, Lowell A.
    Track is for me.

    (The Sports for Me Books)
    SUMMARY: Ron details his experiences participating in practice with his track team and in competing at a meet.

    1. Track-athletics—Juvenile literature. [1. Track and field] I. Oddie, Alan. II. Title. III. Series.

GV1061.D5 1979   796.4'26   79-1508
ISBN 0-8225-1083-9

Manufactured in the United States of America

International Standard Book Number: 0-8225-1083-9
Library of Congress Catalog Card Number: 79-1508

    4   5   6   7   8   9   10   85

Hi! I'm Ron. I want to be a track star. That's not such a crazy idea because I come from a track-minded family. My dad was once a mile runner in college. Casey, my older brother, is a long jumper at the University of California. And my sister Lela is a sprinter, or short-distance runner, at her high school.

"Track" is a short name for the sport of track and field. The sport is really made up of many different kinds of competitions. There are running, jumping, and throwing events.

I have always liked to run, and I am pretty good at throwing and jumping too. So when I became ten years old, I joined the Panthers track team. It has special classes for different age groups, and we compete with children our own age from other city track teams.

Before I joined the Panthers team, I had to go to a doctor for a checkup. He signed a paper saying I was healthy. My parents and I took the health form to the youth center when I signed up for the team.

We also had to pay a registration fee. The fee covered the cost of insurance and uniforms for our track meets.

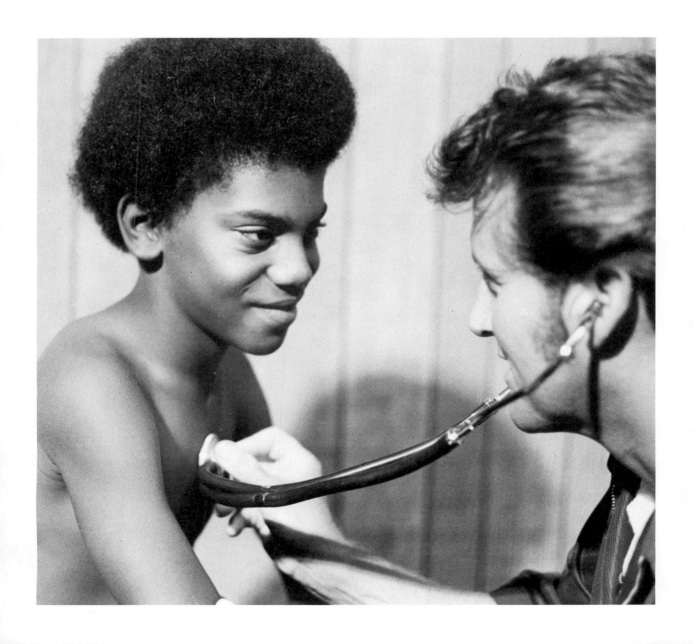

Panthers had to provide their own running shoes. My first pair had rippled rubber soles, but I soon started wearing **spikes** too. Spikes are special track shoes with metal points sticking out of the soles. These points bite into the ground to prevent slipping and sliding.

Younger runners and persons just starting out in track do not wear spikes because they might hurt themselves on the sharp points.

The Panthers practiced at a local high
school. Coach Davis began each practice
with a warm-up period. We twisted. We
stretched. We bent. We did exercises, like
push-ups and sit-ups. But most of all, we
ran. "Running," Coach Davis said, "is the
basis of track."

We worked out on a big oval path called a **track**. It was 440 yards (a quarter mile) around. The track was marked off into smaller lanes. During races, runners start in different lanes. Short-distance runners, or sprinters, cannot step out of their lanes for an entire race. Long-distance runners can cross over into the inside lanes during a race.

The Panthers practiced for two weeks before our first meet. At meets, each of us was allowed to compete in as many as four different events. That meant that at practices, we had to spend time learning the special skills needed for several running, jumping, and throwing events.

I soon learned that there is a lot more to running a race than you might think. In the first place, there are four different kinds of races: sprints, longer distances, hurdles, and relays. And each kind of race takes special running skills.

Sprints are short-distance races of usually 100 or 200 yards or meters. But just because you don't have to run far doesn't mean that sprints are easy! You have to run at top speed for the entire race. In fact, sprints are sometimes called **dashes** because you dash from the start to the finish line.

To help sprinters get an extra-fast start, **starting blocks** are used. The racers rest their feet against the blocks and push off from them at the start of a race. The blocks are anchored to the ground so they won't move when they are pushed against. The push-off start helps sprinters reach top speed quickly.

Because a good start is so important, the Panthers spent a lot of time learning how to use the starting blocks. Coach Davis showed us the different body positions used at different phases of an official start.

When Coach Davis said, "On your marks," I settled firmly against the blocks and rested on one knee. One foot was forward and the other was back at a comfortable distance. I put my hands apart and rested the tips of my fingers just behind the starting line. I tried to relax.

When the coach said, "Get set," I brought my knee up off the ground. I raised my hips so that I leaned forward. My arms supported part of my weight. I held my breath and did not move as I waited for the final signal.

"Go!" I lifted my hands off the ground and pushed forward out of the blocks. I stayed low to the ground until I reached top speed. Even during practices, we sprinted the entire race distance. Coach Davis said that in every race, we should run at top speed past the finish line. He warned us that many races are lost by runners who ease up a step or two before the finish.

Split-second starts are not as important in distance races because you have more time to make up for a bad start. So long-distance racers, like milers, usually do not use starting blocks. They begin from a standing start instead.

Longer races are also run differently than

sprints. Instead of sprinting at top speed, distance runners set a slower **pace**. Your pace should be a comfortable stride at good speed. But you should save enough energy for a strong finish, or **kick**.

Running hurdles takes a different kind of skill. Hurdles are really small fences block-

ing the lanes of a track. Good hurdlers do not jump over the hurdles. They step over them without losing their stride. They lean forward and stretch their legs. You have to be careful not to hook a hurdle with your trailing foot. Point your foot out, not down.

Relay races are unlike other races in which one person runs the entire race. In a relay race, a four-person team divides the distance into four parts called **legs**. Each person runs one leg of the race.

The runners in a relay race carry a **baton**, which is a hollow, plastic tube. When a runner finishes a leg, he or she must pass the baton to the next runner. The worst thing you can do in a relay race is drop the baton. That is why Coach Davis had us practice the baton pass over and over again.

The baton must be passed inside a specially marked **passing zone**. The passing zone is a 22-yard stretch at the end of each runner's leg of the race. If you overrun the zone before the baton is passed, you will have **fouled**. This means that your relay team is out of the race.

Passing takes good timing. When the in-coming runner is still about 10 yards away, you begin to run into the passing zone. You should have picked up speed by the time the baton reaches your hand.

There are two ways to actually pass the baton. Long-distance relay runners usually use the **visual pass**. As the pass receiver picks up speed in the passing zone, he or she looks back and reaches for the baton.

Sprinters usually use the **blind pass**. It is a faster method of passing the baton. But it is also harder to learn. For the blind pass, the receiver does not look back. Instead, he or she thrusts one hand back, palm up. The incoming runner must put the baton right into the upturned hand. Because the receiver doesn't watch the exchange, it is easier to drop the baton.

After learning about the different running events, I decided to enter three at our first track meet. I planned to run in the 100-yard sprint, the 440-yard run, and the 440-yard relay. I chose the long jump for my field event. My brother Casey had been helping me train for that one.

The long jump takes both running and jumping skills. It is important to reach full speed on the run before the jump. You should keep an even stride. Casey showed me how to use markers to help me judge my stride. My markers were pieces of wood. I set them along the runway. I put one marker on the spot where I would begin my run. I put the other marker about two-thirds of the way down the runway. I knew that if I put my right foot down beside this marker, I would be in proper stride for the takeoff into the pit. On my last step, I would hit the takeoff board just right. I wouldn't overstep it and foul out.

Just before reaching the takeoff board, I started lowering my body a little. Casey said I should feel like a cat getting ready to spring. My last step came down firmly on the takeoff board. I straightened my knee and sprang forward into the air.

While in the air, I folded in the middle and snapped my legs and arms forward. I landed in the sand heels first. I fell forward so that no part of my body would touch the sand behind my heel marks. You can lose inches on your jump by falling backward when you land.

At each practice, I felt myself getting better. I looked forward to my first track meet. The Panthers would be competing against the Westlake Hawks.

At the last practice before our meet, Coach Davis gave us some advice. "Eat lightly before a meet," he said. "And don't fill up with water or soft drinks before you race. You might get cramps. Don't chew gum. You might choke. Try to think of yourselves as panthers. The swiftest panthers are the hungry panthers."

Coach Davis also told us to get to the meet early. "Find out what time your events take place and be at the start on time. Warm up in the periods between your competitions."

"Be alert," he said. "Don't wander onto the track during a race. Always watch out for other competitors."

The day of the meet was nice and sunny. Many of our families came to watch. Mom and Dad were in the stands.

I wanted to do my best to help the Panthers win. In track, the winner of an event is awarded five points. Second place gets three points. And third place gets one point. The team with the most points at the end of the day wins the track meet.

I was nervous as I got ready for my first race, the 100-yard dash. I picked up some starting blocks and went to my lane.

The official starter came over and talked to the racers. He told us not to jump the gun. That meant that no one could move out of the blocks before the starting gun went off. If someone got a head start, the race would have to start over again. Anyone who jumped the gun twice would foul out.

We went back into our lanes and settled into our blocks. "On your marks! Get set!"

Bang!

I pushed out of the blocks as hard as I could. As I gained speed, I tried to remember to move in a straight line. I kept my eyes and my toes pointed forward. My arms

were swinging back and forth at my sides. I ran on the balls of my feet and lifted my knees high to lengthen my stride.

Suddenly I felt my fingernails digging into my palms. "Relax," I told myself. I loosened my fists. That helped.

I crossed the finish line at top speed. But top speed wasn't good enough. I came in fourth. And fourth place didn't win any points for the Panthers. I was disappointed, but I remembered to be a good sport. I went over to the winner and shook his hand.

Later that morning, I ran the 440-yard run. It was one full circle, or **lap**, around the track. This time I came in third place. I earned my first point for the Panthers. It was a great feeling!

I had some time before the long-jump competition. So I stopped a minute to watch the high jump. In this event, jumpers try to jump up and over a crossbar. My friend Karen was just getting ready for her second try over the crossbar.

High jumpers can take up to three tries to go over the crossbar at any one height. If they make it over without knocking down the crossbar, it is raised to a new height.

The crossbar for Karen's jump was just over her head. Karen stood back on the grass about 20 yards from the crossbar. She rocked back and forth to build up her rhythm and get in the right mood. She was concentrating so hard that she didn't even notice me.

Then Karen started loping, or running slowly, to the bar. She went in from the right side, making a circling approach. As she neared her takeoff spot, Karen speeded up. Springing upward, she twisted so that her back was toward the crossbar. This kind of jump is called the **flop**.

As Karen's head went over the bar, she

drew her arms in close to her body. For a moment, it looked like her hips might brush the bar. But she kicked her heels out and upward, and she cleared the bar.

Everyone cheered. Karen looked up and grinned. What a jump! If the rest of the jumpers could not match it, she would take first place. Five more points for the Panthers!

On the way to the long-jump pit, I saw Carlos get ready for the shot put. Carlos was the only Panther in the event. He stood in the throwing circle with his back to the throwing field.

Carlos cradled the shot in his right hand. He carried it with his finger tips. Then he tucked the shot next to his jaw by his neck.

Carlos stood still for a moment, balancing himself. Suddenly he bent forward on one leg. He took two quick hops backward on the leg. Then he started to twirl forward. As

he spun around to face the throwing field, he shoved the shot outward. He straightened his arm and body at the same time. The shot sailed through the air. Carlos danced a little on his right foot to keep his balance. He did not step out of the throwing circle.

The heavy shot landed. One of the judges quickly marked the spot where the shot made a dent in the grass. Then he measured the distance with a long tape. While Carlos waited, he looked over and smiled at me. He seemed pleased. I sure was. It was a good put.

Not it was time for the long-jump event. I moved over to the long-jump pit. I took a little time to make a few practice runs along the runway. I set my markers and tried to loosen up.

Soon the judge called my name. I went to my starting marker. Then, like Karen had done, I rocked back and forth a few times to get my rhythm. I looked toward the pit and thought about my jump.

I started forward and got into my stride. I soared out over the pit. It was a good jump. I felt it.

I had two more tries to better my first jump. But the first was my best one. I took second place and won three points.

As the day went on, the track meet was "nip and tuck." The Panthers would have to place first in the last two events to win.

The Panthers' best runner, Janey, was running in the girls' half-mile race. Coach Davis told Janey to stick to her own pace.

"Don't fall into the habit of being a 'rabbit,'" said Coach Davis. "Sometimes fast runners do not save enough energy for a strong finish. If you run like they do, you might burn yourself out."

As the gun sounded, the girls sped down the track. Halfway through the race, Janey was still behind the leader. I wondered whether she was fast enough to win. But then in the final stretch, Janey put out everything she had. With a burst of speed, she overtook the Westlake runner. Janey broke the tape to win.

There was just one event left. It was the 440-yard relay. I was running the third leg. I went to my position halfway around the track.

Soon I heard the starter's gun crack on the opposite side of the field. Two sprinters

raced side by side into the first turn. I saw the batons flashing in their hands as they pumped their arms up and down to gain speed. In no time at all, they were making their first pass.

On the handoff, the Westlake runner bobbled the baton. But then he got a good grip on it and kept coming. Red Murphy, the Panthers' second runner, was speeding toward me.

When Red was about ten yards away, I started forward. I heard Red's footsteps, but I didn't look back. My right hand was straight

out behind me, ready to receive the pass.

We were getting close to the end of the passing zone. I was getting worried. I still did not feel the baton.

Then Red slapped the baton firmly into my hand. I wrapped my fingers around it. Now it was just a case of running as fast as I could.

Sammy Furman was our **anchor man**, or
the last runner in the relay. He was the
fastest runner on our relay team. Sammy
was looking back, waiting for me.

My lungs were burning. And the Westlake
runner was taking the lead. I had almost
finished my leg when Sammy turned around
and took off. He was going so fast that I

was afraid I would not be able to get the baton to him. I was out of breath.

"Wait," I yelled. Sammy slowed down enough for me to slap the baton into his hand. Then he took off down the final leg.

From the cheering of the crowd, I could tell that the race was over. But I couldn't tell who had won. I trotted down to the

finish line. There I found out that Westlake
had won. The Panthers had lost the meet.

Even though we had lost, it had been an
exciting day. The Panthers did not win the
team trophy, but each of us did win ribbons
for placing in the different events. My
family and friends were proud of me. And I
was on my way to becoming a track star!

Words about TRACK

ANCHOR: The runner of the final leg of a relay race

BATON: A hollow, plastic tube that is passed by runners in a relay race

BLIND PASS: A pass used by sprinters in which the pass receiver does not look back but reaches back and receives the baton in his or her upturned hand

DEAD HEAT: A tie at the finish line that occurs when two runners cross the line at the same time

FIELD EVENTS: Jumping and throwing competitions

FLOP: A method of high jumping in which the jumper goes over with his or her back up to the crossbar

HEAT: A preliminary race to eliminate slower competition from a second and final race

HITCH KICK: A motion during the long jump. It looks like the jumper is walking in the air.

KICK: A strong burst of speed at the end of a race

LAP: Once around the track; also called *full circle*

LEG: The distance over which one runner of a relay race must run

MEDLEY RELAY: A relay in which each member of the team runs a different distance

PACE: Each runner's own steady stride

PASSING ZONE: A 22-yard stretch at the end of each relay runner's leg of a race when the baton must be passed on to the next runner

RELAY: A race during which several runners participate as a team

SPRINT: A short-distance race at high speed; also called *dash*

STAGGERED STARTS: A starting formation that is arranged in a jagged form around a curve so that all runners run the same distance

TRIPLE JUMP: A field event in which contestants hop, step, and jump for distance

VISUAL PASS: A pass used by long-distance runners in which the pass receiver looks back at the upcoming runner when he or she reaches for the baton

ABOUT THE AUTHOR

LOWELL A. DICKMEYER is active in athletics as a participant, instructor, and writer. He is particularly interested in youth sport programs, and each summer he organizes sports camps for hundreds of youngsters. Mr. Dickmeyer has been a college physical education instructor and an elementary school principal in southern California.

ABOUT THE PHOTOGRAPHER

ALAN ODDIE was born and raised in Scotland. He now resides in Santa Monica, California. In addition to his work as a photographer, Mr. Oddie is an author and a producer of educational filmstrips. He is currently the staff photographer for *Franciscan Communications*.